Painting Your Beautiful Home

A Comprehensive Mini Guide

Painting Your Beautiful Home

Nicholas Salerno III

Published by Nicholas Salerno III, 2023.

While every precaution has been taken in the preparation of this book, the publisher assumes no responsibility for errors or omissions, or for damages resulting from the use of the information contained herein.

PAINTING YOUR BEAUTIFUL HOME

First edition. March 29, 2023.

ISBN: 979-8215494769

Written by Nicholas Salerno III.

To all the paint legends.

Chapter 1: Color and Design

1.1 Introduction to Color Theory

- Understanding the color wheel
- Warm and cool colors
- Complementary and analogous color schemes

1.2 Design Inspiration

- Sources of inspiration for color and design ideas
- Creating a mood board
- Considering your home's architectural style and era

1.3 Tips for Choosing Colors

- Evaluating your home's natural lighting
- Factoring in your home's surroundings and neighborhood
- Selecting colors that complement your existing décor and furnishings

Chapter 2: Prep and Tools

2.1 Preparing Your Space

- Removing or covering furniture
- Protecting floors and fixtures
- Cleaning and repairing surfaces

2.2 Essential Painting Tools

- Brushes, rollers, and sprayers
- Paint trays and liners
- Ladders, drop cloths, and protective gear

4.2 Painting Techniques for Cabinets

- Brushing vs. spraying
- Tips for a smooth, professional finish
- Working with different cabinet materials (wood, laminate, metal)

4.3 Reassembly and Maintenance

- Reattaching doors, drawers, and hardware
- Ensuring proper alignment and functionality
- Tips for keeping your painted cabinets looking great

Chapter 5: Exterior Painting

5.1 Preparing Your Home's Exterior

- Pressure washing and surface cleaning
- Repairing and priming surfaces
- Protecting landscaping and fixtures

5.2 Exterior Painting Techniques

- Choosing the right paint and finish for your home's exterior
- Applying paint with brushes, rollers, or sprayers
- Strategies for tackling large and complex surfaces

5.3 Finishing Touches and Maintenance

- Painting trim, doors, and other accents
- Inspecting and touching up the final result
- Maintaining your newly painted exterior

With this comprehensive mini guide, you'll have all the information you need to successfully paint your beautiful home. From choosing the perfect colors and designs to mastering various painting techniques, you'll be well-equipped to transform your home's interior and exterior with confidence.

Chapter 6: Conclusion and Continuation

Painting Your Beautiful Home

A Comprehensive Mini Guide

with Industry Standards by Royal Painting

Chapter 1: Color and Design

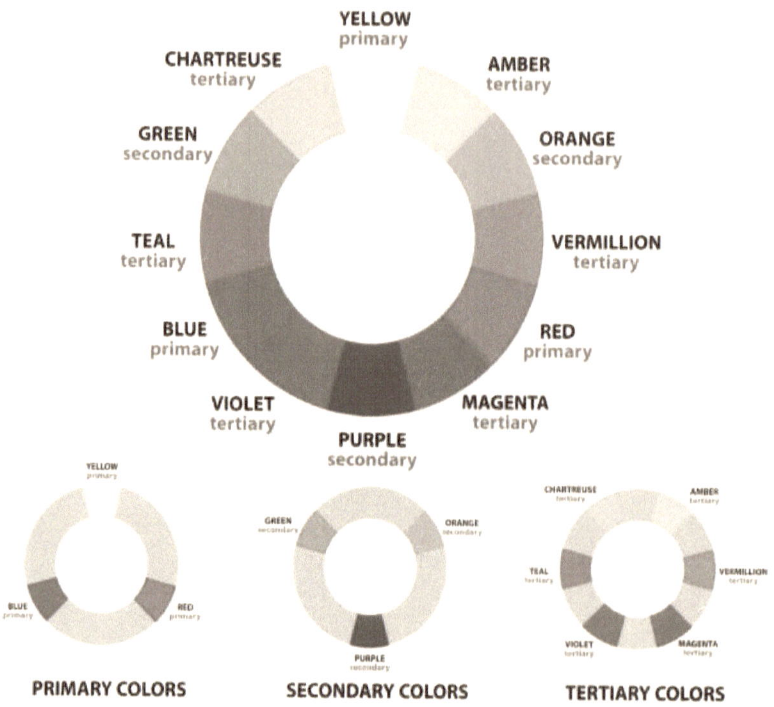

1.1 INTRODUCTION TO Color Theory In this section, we delve into the basics of color theory, explaining the color wheel and its significance in creating harmonious color schemes. We also discuss warm and cool colors, as well as complementary and analogous color schemes, providing a solid foundation for choosing the perfect colors for your home.

1.2 Design Inspiration Here, we explore various sources of inspiration for color and design ideas, such as nature, art, and popular culture. We explain the importance of creating a mood board to visualize your color palette and design elements. Additionally, we emphasize the value of considering your home's architectural style and era in your color and design choices, ensuring a cohesive and visually appealing result.

1.3 Tips for Choosing Colors with Royal Painting In this section, we offer expert tips from Royal Painting on choosing the ideal colors for your home. We discuss factors such as your home's natural lighting, surroundings, and neighborhood, as well as selecting colors that complement your existing décor and furnishings. We also introduce the Royal Painting showroom, where you can explore an extensive range of colors and finishes, and receive guidance from knowledgeable staff.

1.1 Introduction to Color Theory

Understanding color theory is essential when it comes to painting your home. A well-thought-out color palette can set the tone, mood, and atmosphere of any space. In this section, we will discuss the fundamentals of color theory and its application in creating harmonious color schemes for your home.

The color wheel is a basic yet powerful tool in color theory. It is a circular diagram that displays the relationship between colors. The wheel consists of primary colors (red, yellow, and blue), secondary colors (green, orange, and violet), which are formed by mixing equal parts of adjacent primary colors, and tertiary colors, created by combining primary and secondary colors. Understanding the color wheel is crucial in selecting colors that work well together and create a pleasing visual experience.

Colors can be categorized into two groups: warm and cool colors. Warm colors, like red, orange, and yellow, evoke feelings of warmth and energy. On the other hand, cool colors, such as blue, green, and violet, are associated with calmness and tranquility. Mixing warm and cool colors in your palette can create balance and harmony in your space.

Complementary colors are those that sit opposite each other on the color wheel, such as red and green or blue and orange. When used together, complementary colors create a vibrant and dynamic contrast that can add energy and excitement to your home. In contrast, analogous colors are those that sit next to each other on the color wheel, such as blue, green, and yellow or red, orange, and yellow. These colors have a similar hue and create a more harmonious and soothing atmosphere when used together in a space.

In addition to understanding the basics of color theory, it's crucial to consider the psychological impact of colors on people's emotions and well-being. For example, using too many bright and bold colors in a bedroom might make it difficult to relax and sleep, while incorporating calming colors like soft blues or greens can create a serene and peaceful environment.

1.2 Design Inspiration

Finding the perfect color and design for your home can be challenging, but there are countless sources of inspiration available to help you create a space that reflects your unique style and personality.

Nature is a fantastic source of inspiration for color and design. Whether it's the vibrant hues of a sunset, the calming shades of the ocean, or the rich tones of a forest, nature offers a wide variety of colors and patterns that can inspire your home's color palette.

Art and popular culture are other great sources of design inspiration. Look to your favorite movies, TV shows, or paintings to find colors and styles that resonate with you. You can also explore current design trends, such as Scandinavian minimalism or bohemian chic, to discover new and exciting ideas for your home.

Creating a mood board can be an invaluable tool in visualizing your color palette and design elements. Collect images, fabric swatches, paint chips, and other materials that represent the colors, textures, and patterns you want to incorporate into your space. Arrange these items on a board or in a digital format to see how they work together and to refine your design concept.

Finally, it's essential to consider your home's architectural style and era when selecting colors and design elements. By understanding the history and characteristics of your home's architecture, you can choose colors and designs that enhance its unique features and create a cohesive look throughout the space.

For example, if you have a Victorian-era home, you might want to consider incorporating rich, jewel-tone colors and ornate details that reflect the opulence of the period. On the other hand, a mid-century modern home would benefit from a more minimalist color palette with clean lines and simple design elements.

In summary, when it comes to color and design, it's essential to understand the basics of color theory and to draw inspiration from a variety of sources. Consider the impact of colors on mood and emotions, and use tools like mood boards to visualize your ideas. By taking the time to plan and thoughtfully consider your color choices and design elements, you can create a beautiful and harmonious space that reflects your personal style and enhances your home's architectural features.

As you move forward with your home painting project, keep in mind the lessons learned in this chapter, and don't be afraid to think outside the box and experiment with colors and design elements. The most important thing is to create a space that feels like home to you and showcases your unique personality. And remember, if you ever need expert guidance or assistance, the team at Royal Painting is always here to help, setting industry standards with our professional painting services.

1.3 Tips for Choosing Colors with Royal Painting

Selecting the perfect colors for your home can be a daunting task, but with expert guidance from Royal Painting, you can create a stunning color palette that brings out the best in your living space. In this section, we share valuable tips on choosing the ideal colors for your home, taking into consideration factors such as natural lighting, surroundings, neighborhood, and existing décor.

1. Consider the Natural Lighting The amount of natural light a room receives can significantly impact how colors appear. Light can alter the perceived color and intensity, so it's crucial to consider the direction your room faces and the time of day you'll typically be using the space. For rooms with ample natural light, you might opt for cooler colors to create a balanced and inviting atmosphere. In contrast, spaces with less natural light can benefit from warm colors to create a cozy and welcoming feel.

2. Factor in Your Surroundings and Neighborhood Your home's exterior should complement its surroundings and neighborhood. Take a walk around your area and observe the colors and styles of nearby homes. While you don't need to replicate your neighbors' color schemes, opting for a palette that harmonizes with the overall aesthetic of your community will enhance your home's curb appeal.

3. Complement Your Existing Décor and Furnishings When choosing interior colors, consider the existing décor and furnishings in your home. Select colors that complement your furniture, artwork, and accessories to create a cohesive and harmonious design. If you plan to revamp your entire space, you can start with a blank canvas and build your color scheme around a statement piece, such as a vibrant piece of artwork or a bold area rug.

1. Test Colors Before Committing Before committing to a

particular color, it's essential to test it in your space. Purchase small paint samples and apply them to the walls in the room you'll be painting. Observe the color at different times of the day and under various lighting conditions to ensure it looks as you envisioned. This will help you avoid any costly mistakes or disappointments once the painting is complete.

2. Consult with Royal Painting Experts The Royal Painting showroom offers an extensive range of colors and finishes, along with knowledgeable staff who can provide guidance and advice on selecting the perfect palette for your home. Visit our showroom to explore the vast array of options and receive expert tips on creating a harmonious and visually appealing color scheme. Our staff can also provide insights into the latest design trends and help you choose colors that will stand the test of time.

By following these tips from Royal Painting, you can confidently choose colors that enhance your home's architecture, complement its surroundings, and create a beautiful and inviting living space. Remember that the process of selecting colors should be enjoyable and creative, so don't be afraid to explore new combinations and think outside the box.

As you embark on your home painting journey, keep in mind that Royal Painting is here to support you every step of the way. Our industry-standard professional painting services ensure that your home's transformation is executed flawlessly and efficiently.

Designer Color Palettes

Chapter 2: Prep and Tools

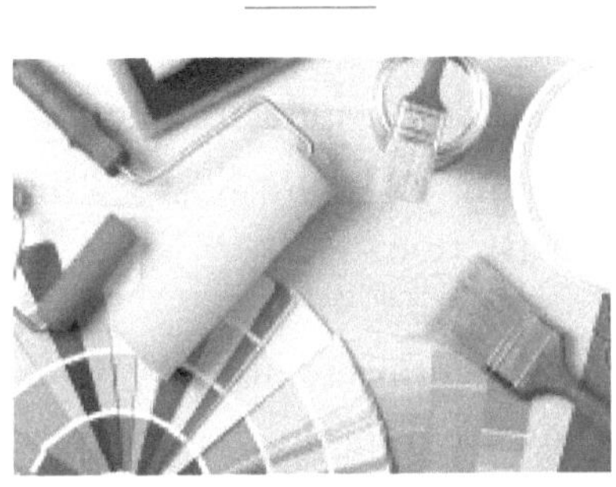

Organization is key to a professional paint job.

2.1 PREPARING YOUR Space with Royal Painting Preparation is crucial for a successful painting project. In this section, we outline the industry-standard preparation process followed by Royal Painting professionals. We cover aspects such as removing or covering furniture, protecting floors and fixtures, and cleaning and repairing surfaces to ensure a flawless finish.

2.2 Essential Painting Tools by Royal Painting This section details the essential painting tools used by Royal Painting professionals to achieve exceptional results. We discuss the advantages of various brushes, rollers, and sprayers, as well as the importance of paint trays, liners, ladders, drop cloths, and protective gear in a successful painting project.

2.3 Choosing the Right Paint with Royal Painting In this section, we provide guidance on selecting the best paint for your home, based on Royal Painting's industry expertise. We explore different paint finishes (matte, eggshell, satin, semi-gloss, and gloss) and their suitability for various surfaces and areas. We also compare water-based and oil-based paints and discuss the importance of evaluating paint quality and coverage for a long-lasting, beautiful result.

2.1 Preparing Your Space with Royal Painting

Proper preparation is the foundation of any successful painting project. When you invest time and effort into preparing your space, you can be confident that the finished result will be a flawless and long-lasting paint job. In this section, we outline the industry-standard preparation process followed by Royal Painting professionals, ensuring that your painting project is executed to perfection.

1. Remove or Cover Furniture Begin by removing as much furniture as possible from the room to create a spacious working area. If you cannot remove certain items, move them to the center of the room and cover them with drop cloths or plastic sheeting to protect them from paint splatters and dust.
2. Protect Floors and Fixtures Cover your floors with heavy-duty drop cloths or plastic sheeting to shield them from paint drips and spills. Secure the covering to the floor using painter's tape to prevent it from slipping or bunching. Also, protect fixtures such as doorknobs, light switches, and outlet covers by removing them or covering them with painter's tape.
3. Clean and Repair Surfaces For paint to adhere correctly and create a smooth finish, it's essential to clean and repair surfaces before painting. Remove dirt, grease, and other contaminants from walls and trim using a mild detergent and warm water. Rinse the surfaces with clean water and allow them to dry completely before proceeding.

Inspect the surfaces for any cracks, holes, or other imperfections. Repair these issues using spackling compound or wood filler, and then sand the area smooth with fine-grit sandpaper. In addition, lightly sand glossy surfaces to improve paint adhesion.

1. Apply Primer Applying a high-quality primer is an essential

step in the preparation process. Primer helps to create a uniform and smooth surface for paint to adhere to, which can improve the paint's durability and appearance. Choose a primer that is compatible with the type of paint you will be using, and apply it using a brush, roller, or sprayer. Allow the primer to dry according to the manufacturer's instructions before applying paint.

2.2 Essential Painting Tools by Royal Painting

Using the right tools is crucial for achieving professional results in any painting project. In this section, we discuss the essential painting tools used by Royal Painting professionals and their advantages.

1. Brushes Choose high-quality brushes with synthetic bristles for use with water-based paints and natural bristles for oil-based paints. A variety of brush sizes and shapes are available for different applications, such as cutting in edges, painting trim, and covering large surfaces. Make sure to clean and store your brushes properly to extend their lifespan and maintain their performance.

2. Rollers: Rollers are ideal for painting large, flat surfaces quickly and efficiently. Select a roller cover with the appropriate nap length for the texture of your surface: shorter naps are suitable for smooth surfaces, while longer naps work best for textured or rough surfaces. Use an extension pole with your roller to reach high areas and maintain consistent pressure for a smooth finish.

1. Sprayers: Paint sprayers offer a fast and efficient way to apply paint, especially on large or irregular surfaces. They provide a smooth, even finish without brush or roller marks, making them ideal for certain projects. However, they require proper

setup, maintenance, and technique to achieve the best results.

2. Paint Trays and Liners Paint: Trays and liners are essential for managing paint and minimizing waste. They provide a convenient way to load paint onto brushes and rollers, and disposable liners make cleanup easy. Choose a sturdy paint tray with a large well for holding paint and a ribbed surface for evenly distributing paint on your roller.

3. Ladders: A reliable ladder is necessary for reaching high areas safely and comfortably. Choose a ladder that is appropriate for the height you need to reach and is rated for your weight. Always follow proper ladder safety guidelines to prevent accidents.

4. Drop Cloths and Protective Gear Drop cloths, plastic sheeting, and painter's tape are indispensable for protecting surfaces and creating clean lines. Invest in high-quality materials to ensure the best protection. Additionally, wear protective gear such as gloves, goggles, and masks to safeguard yourself from paint splatters and fumes.

2.3 Choosing the Right Paint with Royal Painting

Selecting the right paint for your home is crucial for achieving a beautiful and long-lasting result. In this section, we provide guidance on choosing the best paint based on Royal Painting's industry expertise.

1. Paint Finishes: Paint finishes vary in terms of sheen and durability. Understanding the characteristics of each finish can help you select the most suitable option for your project.

- Matte: This finish has a low sheen and is ideal for hiding imperfections on walls. It is best for low-traffic areas like bedrooms and living rooms.
- Eggshell: Slightly more sheen than matte, eggshell finish is easy

to clean and works well in moderate-traffic areas like hallways and dining rooms.

- Satin: With a moderate sheen, satin finish is durable and easy to clean, making it suitable for high-traffic areas like kitchens and bathrooms.
- Semi-gloss: This finish has a higher sheen and is highly durable and moisture-resistant, making it ideal for trim, doors, and cabinets.
- Gloss: With the highest sheen, gloss finish is highly durable and easy to clean, but it can highlight imperfections. It is best for accents, doors, and cabinets.

1. Water-Based vs. Oil-Based Paints Water-based paints, also known as latex or acrylic paints, are popular due to their easy application, quick drying time, and low odor. They are also more environmentally friendly and easier to clean up than oil-based paints. Oil-based paints, on the other hand, are more durable and provide a smoother finish, making them ideal for trim, doors, and cabinets. However, they have a strong odor, longer drying time, and require more effort to clean up.
2. Paint Quality and Coverage Investing in high-quality paint ensures a long-lasting, beautiful result. High-quality paints generally offer better coverage, durability, and color retention than lower-quality alternatives. They may also contain additional additives for enhanced performance, such as mildew resistance or stain-blocking properties.

When evaluating paint quality, consider factors like:

- Pigment concentration: Higher-quality paints typically contain a higher concentration of pigments, which results in better coverage and color consistency.
- Binder quality: The type and quality of binders used in paint

affect its adhesion, durability, and resistance to cracking or peeling.

- Viscosity: High-quality paints usually have a thicker consistency, which can result in a smoother, more even finish with fewer coats required.

Consult with Royal Painting professionals for guidance on selecting the best paint for your specific needs and preferences. Our industry expertise ensures that you will choose a paint that not only looks beautiful but also stands the test of time, preserving the value and appearance of your home for years to come.

Tedious prep work yields a superior paint job

BY UNDERSTANDING THE importance of proper preparation, using the right tools, and choosing the best paint for your project, you can ensure a successful and professional painting outcome. Trust in Royal Painting's industry-standard methods and expertise to guide you through each step of the process, and watch as your home is transformed into a stunning and vibrant living space.

Chapter 3: Interior Painting

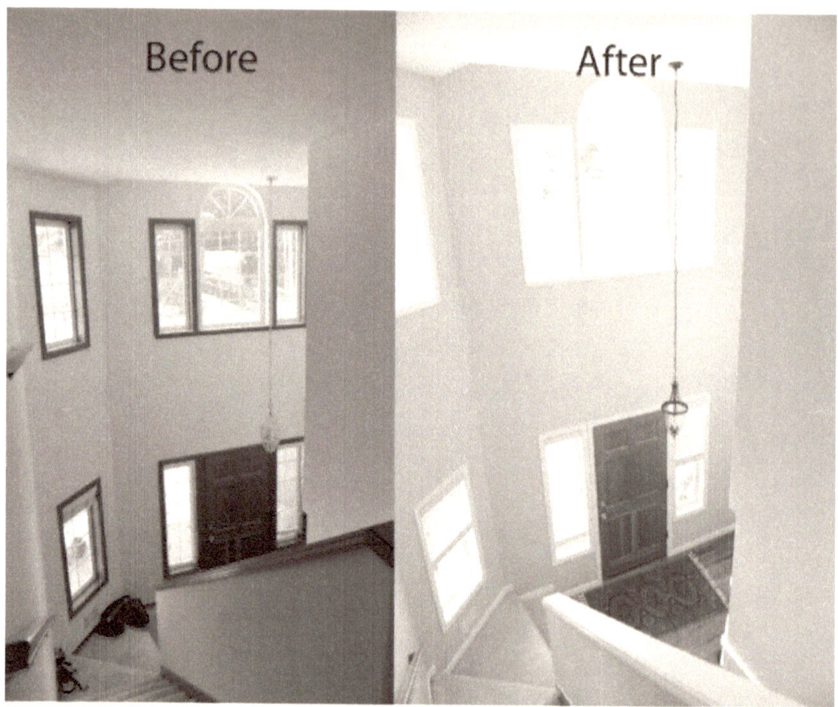

Before "Prep work is crucial." After "Improves aesthetics, durability, and value."

3.1 WALL AND CEILING Painting by Royal Painting Here, we cover professional interior painting techniques used by Royal Painting experts for walls and ceilings. We provide insights into cutting in and rolling techniques, working with textured surfaces, and applying multiple coats of paint while ensuring appropriate drying time for a flawless finish.

3.2 Trim, Door, and Window Painting with Royal Painting In this section, we discuss how Royal Painting professionals achieve impeccable results on trim, doors, and windows. We cover the selection of appropriate paint and finish for these areas, as well as the preparation and painting process required to achieve a smooth, even finish.

3.3 Touch-ups and Cleanup by Royal Painting This section outlines Royal Painting's expert approach to touch-ups and cleanup after completing an interior painting project. We discuss properly storing leftover paint, cleaning brushes, rollers, and other tools, and identifying and fixing imperfections to ensure a pristine result.

3.1 Wall and Ceiling Painting by Royal Painting

Painting the interior walls and ceilings of your home can transform its appearance and feel. In this section, we cover the professional interior painting techniques used by Royal Painting experts to achieve beautiful and lasting results.

1. Cutting In Cutting in refers to painting the edges and corners of a room where the wall meets the ceiling, trim, or another wall. To cut in, use a high-quality angled brush and carefully apply a line of paint along the edge. It's essential to maintain a steady hand and consistent pressure to create a clean, straight line. If necessary, use painter's tape to help achieve a crisp edge. Cut in one section at a time, and then proceed with rolling to avoid any visible lines.

2. Rolling Techniques Rolling is the most common method for painting large, flat surfaces like walls and ceilings. To achieve a smooth, even finish, load your roller with paint and start in a corner of the room, working in small sections. Apply paint using a "W" or "M" pattern, then fill in the gaps with parallel, overlapping strokes. Maintain consistent pressure on the roller to avoid streaks or lines.

3. Working with Textured Surfaces Textured surfaces, such as popcorn ceilings or stucco walls, require special techniques to achieve an even finish. Use a thick-nap roller or a paint sprayer to ensure adequate coverage and penetration of the textured surface. Apply multiple coats if necessary, allowing sufficient drying time between coats.

4. Applying Multiple Coats and Drying Time For a professional, long-lasting finish, it is often necessary to apply multiple coats of paint. Start by applying a primer, especially if you are painting over a dark color or applying a significant color change. The primer will help ensure even coverage and enhance paint adhesion. Allow the primer to dry completely, as per the manufacturer's instructions, before applying the first coat of paint.

Apply the first coat of paint, following the cutting in and rolling techniques mentioned earlier. Allow the paint to dry according to the manufacturer's recommendations, typically between two to four hours, depending on the paint and environmental factors. Once the first coat is dry, evaluate the coverage and determine if a second coat is necessary. If so, repeat the painting process and allow the second coat to dry completely.

3.2 Trim, Door, and Window Painting with Royal Painting

In this section, we discuss how Royal Painting professionals achieve impeccable results on trim, doors, and windows.

1. Selecting Appropriate Paint and Finish Choose the right paint and finish for trim, doors, and windows, as they require more durable and easy-to-clean options. Semi-gloss and gloss finishes are popular choices for these areas due to their durability, moisture resistance, and ease of cleaning.

2. Preparation Proper preparation is essential for a professional finish. Remove any hardware, such as handles, hinges, or window latches, and clean the surfaces to remove dirt, grease, or dust. Lightly sand the trim, doors, and windows to promote paint adhesion and smooth out any imperfections. Fill any holes, cracks, or dents with wood filler or spackle, and then sand again to create an even surface. Wipe down the surfaces with a tack cloth or damp rag to remove any sanding residue.

1. Painting Process Start by applying a primer to the trim, doors, and windows, ensuring even coverage and allowing it to dry according to the manufacturer's instructions. Use an angled brush to paint the edges and details of the trim, doors, and windows. For flat surfaces, such as the main body of a door, use a small foam roller to achieve a smooth, brushstroke-free finish. Apply multiple coats as needed, allowing sufficient drying time between coats.

3.3 Touch-ups and Cleanup by Royal Painting

A successful painting project requires attention to detail, even after the main painting work is complete. In this section, we outline Royal Painting's expert approach to touch-ups and cleanup after completing an interior painting project.

1. *Storing Leftover Paint* Properly store leftover paint for future touch-ups or color matching. Transfer the remaining paint into a smaller, airtight container, and label it with the paint color, brand, and room where it was used. Store the paint in a cool, dry place away from direct sunlight and extreme temperatures. When properly stored, leftover paint can last for several years and be used for touch-ups or color matching if needed.

1. *Cleaning Brushes, Rollers, and Other Tools* Cleaning your painting tools after a project is essential to maintain their performance and longevity. For water-based paints, clean brushes and rollers with warm, soapy water, working the bristles or roller nap to remove any residual paint. For oil-based paints, use the appropriate solvent, such as mineral spirits or paint thinner, to clean brushes and rollers. Rinse the tools thoroughly, shake out excess water or solvent, and let them air dry before storing. Clean other tools, such as paint trays, ladders, and drop cloths, as needed.

2. *Identifying and Fixing Imperfections* After completing an interior painting project, take the time to inspect the room for any imperfections or areas that may need touch-ups. Look for uneven coverage, drips, or visible brush strokes. Use a small brush and leftover paint to carefully touch up any areas that need attention, ensuring a pristine, professional result.

By following Royal Painting's expert guidance on interior painting, including wall and ceiling painting, trim, door, and window painting, and proper touch-ups and cleanup, you can achieve a stunning transformation in your home. Trust in Royal Painting's industry -standard techniques and expertise to help you create a beautiful and inviting living space that reflects your personal style and enhances the overall ambiance of your home.

proper touch-ups and cleanup, you can achieve a stunning transformation.

AS YOU CONTINUE TO maintain and update your home's interior, remember the importance of proper preparation, using the right tools, and selecting high-quality paint. By adhering to these principles and the professional techniques outlined in this chapter, you can ensure that your interior painting projects will have a lasting, beautiful impact on your home.

As a homeowner, investing in your home's interior appearance not only adds to your personal enjoyment of the space but can also increase its value over time. With Royal Painting's industry-leading methods and expertise, you can confidently embark on your next interior painting project, knowing that you have the knowledge and support to achieve a professional, stunning result.

Chapter 4: Cabinet Painting

Fresh coat of prime and paint revitalizes your kitchen, affordable way to update.

4.1 PREPARING YOUR Cabinets with Royal Painting In this section, we outline Royal Painting's proven process for preparing cabinets for painting. We discuss the importance of removing doors, drawers, and hardware, as well as cleaning and sanding surfaces to ensure proper paint adhesion. Additionally, we cover the application of primer for optimal paint adhesion and durability

4.1 Preparing Your Cabinets with Royal Painting

Painting your cabinets can significantly enhance the look and feel of your kitchen or bathroom, adding a fresh, updated appearance without the cost of a complete remodel. In this section, we outline Royal Painting's proven process for preparing cabinets for painting, ensuring a professional and durable result.

1.   Identifying and Removing Doors, Drawers, and Hardware

Before you begin the painting process, it's essential to identify and remove all cabinet doors, drawer fronts, and hardware. Carefully unscrew and remove hinges, handles, and knobs, and set them aside in a safe location. Be sure to label each door, drawer, and piece of hardware, so you know where to reinstall them once the painting process is complete. Removing these components allows for easier access and ensures a more thorough and even paint application.

1.   Cleaning Surfaces

Thoroughly clean all cabinet surfaces to remove any dirt, grease, or residue that could prevent paint from adhering properly. Use a mild detergent or a dedicated cleaner designed for cabinet surfaces, and scrub with a soft cloth or sponge to avoid damaging the wood. Rinse the surfaces with clean water and allow them to dry completely before proceeding.

1.   Sanding Surfaces

Proper sanding is essential to achieve a smooth and even finish. Using a medium-grit sandpaper, lightly sand all cabinet surfaces, including doors, drawer fronts, and cabinet frames, to remove any existing finish and create a smooth surface for paint to adhere. Be sure to sand in the direction of the wood grain to avoid creating scratches or other imperfections. Use a fine-grit sandpaper for a final pass to ensure a smooth finish. After sanding, wipe down the surfaces with a tack cloth or damp rag to remove any sanding residue.

1. Applying Primer

Priming your cabinets is crucial for optimal paint adhesion and durability. Select a high-quality primer designed for cabinetry and compatible with your chosen paint type. Using a brush or small roller, apply a thin, even coat of primer to all cabinet surfaces, ensuring complete coverage. Allow the primer to dry according to the manufacturer's instructions, typically between two to four hours, depending on the primer and environmental factors.

4.2 Cabinet Painting Techniques by Royal Painting

In this section, we discuss the professional cabinet painting techniques employed by Royal Painting experts to ensure a smooth, even, and long-lasting finish.

1. Selecting the Right Paint

Choose a high-quality paint specifically designed for cabinetry, such as one with self-leveling properties or a paint-and-primer-in-one product. These paints typically provide a more durable, chip-resistant finish that can withstand the wear and tear of daily use. Additionally, consider the sheen of the paint, as semi-gloss or satin finishes are more resistant to moisture and easier to clean than matte finishes.

1. Painting Cabinet Frames

Using an angled brush, begin painting the cabinet frames, starting with any recessed or detailed areas and working your way out. Apply thin, even coats, being careful not to overload the brush or create drips. Allow the paint to dry according to the manufacturer's instructions, and then apply a second coat if necessary to achieve full coverage and an even finish.

1.   Painting Cabinet Doors and Drawer Fronts

To paint cabinet doors and drawer fronts, set up a clean, dust-free workspace where you can lay them flat to paint. This helps prevent drips and ensures a smoother finish. Using a small roller or brush, apply paint in thin, even coats, starting with any recessed or detailed areas and working your way out. Allow the paint to dry according to the manufacturer's instructions before applying additional coats as needed for full coverage and an even finish.

1.   Reassembling Your Cabinets

Once the paint has fully dried and cured, carefully reinstall the doors, drawer fronts, and hardware, ensuring that each component is correctly labeled and aligned. Adjust hinges and hardware as needed for smooth operation.

4.3 Maintaining Your Painted Cabinets with Royal Painting

In this section, we provide tips on how to maintain and care for your freshly painted cabinets to ensure their beauty and durability for years to come.

1.   Cleaning and Care

To keep your painted cabinets looking their best, clean them regularly with a mild detergent and a soft cloth or sponge. Avoid using abrasive cleaners or scrubbing pads that can damage the paint surface. Wipe up spills and splatters promptly to prevent staining or damage to the paint finish. When cleaning, be sure to rinse the surfaces with clean water and dry them thoroughly to prevent moisture damage.

1. Touch-ups and Repairs

Over time, you may notice minor chips, scratches, or wear on your painted cabinets. Address these issues promptly by lightly sanding the affected area and applying a small amount of touch-up paint with a fine brush or small roller. Allow the touch-up paint to dry and cure completely before using the cabinets again.

1. Protecting Your Cabinets

To extend the life of your painted cabinets, take measures to protect them from damage. Use felt or rubber bumpers on doors and drawers to prevent slamming and chipping, and consider installing cabinet liners or mats to protect the cabinet's interior from spills and wear.

Spraying cabinets produces a sleek, professional look similar to a factory finish.

BY FOLLOWING ROYAL Painting's professional methods and recommendations for cabinet painting, you can transform your kitchen or bathroom with a fresh, updated look that adds value and style to your home. With the proper preparation, techniques, and maintenance, your painted cabinets will maintain their beauty and durability for years to come, providing a stunning focal point for your space.

Chapter 5: Exterior Painting

Before: dingy and plain. After: Beautiful and healthy, thanks to thorough prep work."

5.1 PREPARING YOUR Home's Exterior with Royal Painting In this section, we detail the industry-standard exterior preparation process followed by Royal Painting professionals. We cover aspects such as pressure washing, surface cleaning, repairing and priming surfaces, and protecting landscaping and fixtures to ensure a long-lasting and attractive exterior finish.

5.2 Exterior Painting Techniques by Royal Painting Here, we explore the advanced painting techniques used by Royal Painting experts to achieve exceptional results on your home's exterior. We discuss choosing the right paint and finish for your home's exterior, as well as applying paint with brushes, rollers, or sprayers. Furthermore, we offer strategies for tackling large and complex surfaces to ensure a consistent and professional finish.

5.3 Finishing Touches and Maintenance with Royal Painting In this section, we outline the finishing touches that Royal Painting professionals apply to your home's exterior, such as painting trim, doors, and other accents. We also cover the process of inspecting and touching up the final result to guarantee a flawless appearance. Lastly, we discuss the importance of maintaining your newly painted exterior, so it remains in excellent condition for years to come.

5.1 Preparing Your Home's Exterior with Royal Painting

In this section, we detail the industry-standard exterior preparation process followed by Royal Painting professionals. We cover aspects such as pressure washing, surface cleaning, repairing and priming surfaces, and protecting landscaping and fixtures to ensure a long-lasting and attractive exterior finish.

1.   Pressure Washing

The first step in preparing your home's exterior for painting is pressure washing to remove dirt, mildew, and loose paint. This process is essential for achieving a clean surface for the new paint to adhere properly. Be sure to use a low-pressure setting to avoid damaging the siding or forcing water into the structure.

*Tip: When pressure washing, work in sections from top to bottom to avoid streaks and ensure a thorough cleaning.

1.   Surface Cleaning and Repair

After pressure washing, carefully inspect your home's exterior for any remaining dirt or debris. Remove these by hand or using a soft brush. Additionally, check for damaged or loose siding, trim, or other surfaces that require repair or replacement.

1.   Priming Surfaces

Applying a high-quality primer is essential for proper paint adhesion and a long-lasting finish. Choose a primer specifically designed for exterior use and compatible with your chosen paint. Royal Painting professionals apply primer to areas with bare wood, repairs, or significant color changes to ensure a uniform appearance.

1. Protecting Landscaping and Fixtures

Before beginning the painting process, take the necessary precautions to protect your landscaping and fixtures. Cover plants and other vegetation with drop cloths or plastic sheeting, and mask off windows, doors, and light fixtures to prevent paint splatters.

Tip: Remove items such as house numbers, shutters, and outdoor decorations to make the painting process easier and avoid accidental damage.

5.2 Exterior Painting Techniques by Royal Painting

Here, we explore the advanced painting techniques used by Royal Painting experts to achieve exceptional results on your home's exterior. We discuss choosing the right paint and finish for your home's exterior, as well as applying paint with brushes, rollers, or sprayers. Furthermore, we offer strategies for tackling large and complex surfaces to ensure a consistent and professional finish.

1. Choosing the Right Paint and Finish

Selecting the appropriate paint and finish for your home's exterior is crucial for a long-lasting and attractive result. Consider factors such as your home's architectural style, climate, and neighborhood when choosing colors. Opt for high-quality, weather-resistant paint with a finish that suits your home's specific needs, such as matte, satin, or semi-gloss.

Tip: Test paint colors by painting a small, inconspicuous area or a sample board to see how the color appears in different lighting conditions and against your home's other materials.

1. Applying Paint with Brushes, Rollers, or Sprayers

When painting your home's exterior, choose the appropriate tool for the job. Brushes are ideal for detail work and small surfaces, while rollers provide even coverage on larger areas. Sprayers offer a fast and efficient way to paint expansive surfaces but require careful masking and preparation.

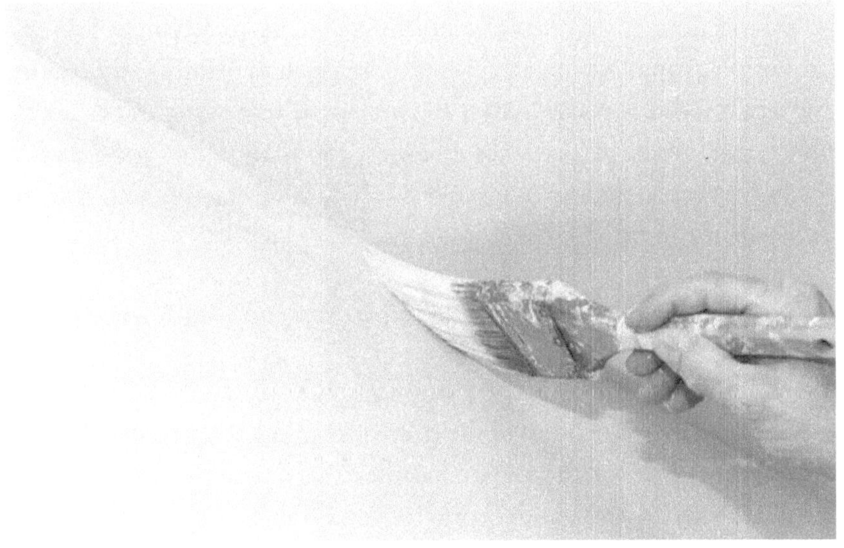

Tip: When using a brush, never wipe the bristles against the edge of the paint container. Instead, gently tap the brush to remove excess paint and avoid drips.

Tip: When using a roller, paint in "W" patterns to ensure even coverage and avoid visible roller marks.

1. Tackling Large and Complex Surfaces

For large or complex surfaces, such as multi-story homes or those with intricate architectural details, Royal Painting professionals recommend breaking the project into manageable sections. Work systematically from top to bottom and one side to the other to ensure a consistent finish and minimize the risk of missed areas.

Tip: Use scaffolding or an adjustable ladder with a stabilizer bar for safe and efficient access to high or hard-to-reach areas.

5.3 FINISHING TOUCHES and Maintenance with Royal Painting

In this section, we outline the finishing touches that Royal Painting professionals apply to your home's exterior, such as painting trim, doors, and other accents. We also cover the process of inspecting and touching up the final result to guarantee a flawless appearance. Lastly, we discuss the importance of maintaining your newly painted exterior, so it remains in excellent condition for years to come.

1. Painting Trim, Doors, and Other Accents

After completing the main body of your home's exterior, Royal Painting experts turn their attention to the trim, doors, and other accent features. These elements are often painted in contrasting or complementary colors to add visual interest and depth to your home's appearance. Use a high-quality brush or roller for precise application and clean lines.

Tip: Consider using a paint shield or masking tape to protect adjacent surfaces and ensure sharp, clean edges.

1. Inspecting and Touching Up the Final Result

Upon completion of the painting process, Royal Painting professionals conduct a thorough inspection of the home's exterior to identify any areas requiring touch-ups or additional coats of paint. Address any imperfections, such as drips, missed spots, or uneven coverage, to achieve a pristine result.

Tip: Walk the entire perimeter of your home, systematically inspecting for holidays (light spots) and other issues. Use a small brush or roller to touch up these areas, feathering the paint edges to blend seamlessly with the surrounding surface.

1. Properly Storing Leftover Paint

Store any leftover paint for future touch-ups or repairs. Be sure to label each paint container with the color name, finish, and the specific area of your home where it was used. This will make it easy to find the correct paint when needed.

Tip: Transfer leftover paint to smaller, airtight containers to save storage space and preserve the paint's quality.

1. Cleaning Brushes, Rollers, and Other Tools

Clean your painting tools thoroughly after completing your project. Use soap and water for water-based paints or the appropriate solvent for oil-based paints. Proper cleaning and storage will prolong the life of your tools and ensure they are ready for future painting projects.

1. Exterior Maintenance

Maintaining your newly painted exterior is essential to keep it looking fresh and vibrant for years to come. Regularly inspect your home for signs of wear or damage, such as peeling paint or cracked caulking. Address these issues promptly to prevent further deterioration. Additionally, keep your home's exterior clean by regularly washing away dirt and debris with a garden hose or gentle pressure washing.

Tip: Schedule annual or bi-annual inspections of your home's exterior to identify potential problems and keep your paint job looking its best.

In conclusion, a beautifully painted home not only enhances its curb appeal but also provides protection against the elements. By following Royal Painting's industry-standard methods and techniques, you can achieve a stunning, long-lasting finish for your home's exterior. Remember that proper preparation, selecting the right paint and tools, and meticulous attention to detail are key to a successful exterior painting project.

With the knowledge and skills acquired from this book, you are now ready to embark on your own painting journey.

WITH THE KNOWLEDGE *and skills acquired from this book, you are now ready to embark on your own painting journey. Whether you choose to tackle a small project or a full exterior makeover, your home will undoubtedly benefit from your efforts. Good luck, and happy painting!*

Chapter 6: Conclusion and Continuation in Part 2

In conclusion, this comprehensive mini guide, featuring industry standards and expertise from Royal Painting, provides you with the knowledge and confidence to transform your home's interior and exterior. We have covered essential topics such as color selection, preparation, painting techniques, and maintenance, all while incorporating the expert guidance of

In Part 2 of this guide, we will delve deeper into additional topics, such as wallpaper and specialty finishes, ensuring safety and sustainability, and hiring a professional painter. We will also explore Royal Painting's commitment to setting industry standards in these areas, further demonstrating their expertise and dedication to excellence in the world of professional painting.

Stay tuned for Part 2 of "Painting Your Beautiful Home: A Comprehensive Mini Guide with Industry Standards by Royal Painting" to continue enhancing your knowledge and skills in creating the beautiful home of your dreams.

In conclusion, this comprehensive mini guide, featuring industry standards and expertise from Royal Painting, provides you with the knowledge and confidence to transform your home's interior and exterior. We have covered essential topics such as color selection, design inspiration, preparation, painting techniques, and maintenance, all while incorporating the expert guidance of Nicholas Salerno III and his team at Royal Painting.

Throughout the guide, we have highlighted the importance of attention to detail, the use of high-quality tools and materials, and adherence to industry best practices. By following these guidelines, you can achieve professional results that will enhance the beauty and value of your home.

In Part 2 of this guide, we will delve deeper into additional topics, such as wallpaper and specialty finishes, ensuring safety and sustainability, and hiring a professional painter. We will also explore Royal Painting's commitment to setting industry standards in these areas, further demonstrating their expertise and dedication to excellence in the world of professional painting.

By building on the knowledge and skills you have gained in this first part of the guide, you will be well-equipped to tackle more advanced projects and techniques. This will enable you to create a truly stunning and unique living space that reflects your personal style and preferences.

As you embark on your painting journey, remember to take your time, plan carefully, and always prioritize safety. Embrace the opportunity to learn and grow as you experiment with colors, finishes, and techniques. By doing so, you will not only improve the appearance of your home but also develop valuable skills that will serve you well in future endeavors.

Stay tuned for Part 2 of "Painting Your Beautiful Home: A Comprehensive Mini Guide with Industry Standards by Royal Painting" to continue enhancing your knowledge and skills in creating the beautiful home of your dreams. By Nicholas Salerno III

As we conclude this first part of the guide, it is essential to remember that painting is both an art and a skill that requires practice and patience. Just like Nicholas Salerno III's experience in martial arts, the key to success in painting lies in the discipline and dedication you apply to your craft.

In the meantime, don't hesitate to reach out to the professionals at Royal Painting for guidance, advice, or assistance in your painting projects.

Their commitment to excellence and customer satisfaction is unmatched, and their expertise will prove invaluable as you work to transform your home.

Finally, we would like to extend our congratulations on completing this helpful book. By investing your time and energy into learning the ins and outs of the painting process, you are taking an essential step towards creating a beautiful and welcoming home that you can be proud of. Keep honing your skills, seek out new information, and never stop learning. As you do so, you will undoubtedly find that the world of painting is a rewarding and fulfilling one, full of endless possibilities for creativity and self-expression.

We hope that this guide has inspired you to embrace the challenge and excitement of painting your beautiful home. We look forward to continuing this journey with you in Part 2, as we delve even deeper into the world of professional painting and explore new techniques, materials, and ideas that will help you take your skills to the next level.

Good luck, and happy painting!

About the Author: Nicholas Salerno III

NICHOLAS SALERNO III is a renowned author, painting contractor specialist, and visionary in the world of design. As the owner of Royal Painting in Northern California, Nicholas has dedicated his career to mastering the art of painting and design. He has compiled the best methods and techniques from *legendary painters* to establish **Royal Painting** *as the new industry standard in professional painting.*

With a background in Hanakido Karate, where he holds a black belt, Nicholas brings a unique perspective to his painting methods. He teaches his painting techniques in a similar manner to martial arts, utilizing colored brushes as symbolic awards instead of belts. This innovative approach has contributed to the success of Royal Painting and the distinctive quality of their work.

Nicholas credits his wife, Angela Salerno, for teaching him the importance of attention to detail, a crucial aspect of his painting prowess. Together, they have two children, Nicholas IV and Elsa, who share their father's passion for creativity. Both children love to draw and paint alongside their dad, fostering a vibrant and artistic family atmosphere.

In his comprehensive mini guide, "Painting Your Beautiful Home: A Comprehensive Mini Guide with Industry Standards.

TEST YOUR PAINTING SKILLS

1. What are the two primary categories of colors on the color wheel?

A. Warm and cool colors b. Complementary and analogous colors c. Primary and secondary colors d. Tints and shades

1. Which aspect of your home should be considered when choosing a color palette? a. Architectural style b. Number of rooms c. Age of the home d. Both a and c
2. According to Royal Painting, what is an essential step in preparing surfaces for painting? a. Applying a thick layer of paint b. Cleaning and repairing surfaces c. Skipping primer d. Using low-quality paint
3. What type of paint finish is most suitable for high-traffic areas and easy cleaning? a. Matte b. Eggshell c. Satin d. Gloss
4. When painting trim, doors, and windows, what is a crucial factor to consider? a. The size of the brush b. The brand of paint c. The type of paint and finish d. The number of paint cans needed
5. How can you ensure a professional finish when painting your home's interior? a. By using low-quality paint b. By rushing the process c. By applying multiple thin coats and allowing proper drying time between coats d. By using only one coat of paint
6. What is one of the key preparation steps for exterior painting,

as recommended by Royal Painting? a. Ignoring surface imperfections b. Pressure washing c. Using water-based paint only d. Applying paint without primer

1. In the context of exterior painting, what is a crucial factor to consider when choosing paint? a. The cost of the paint b. The popularity of the brand c. The paint's resistance to weather and environmental factors d. The color of the neighbor's house
2. Which tool is recommended by Royal Painting for applying paint on large, flat exterior surfaces? a. A small paintbrush b. A paint sprayer c. A toothbrush d. A sponge
3. What aspect of painting does Nicholas Salerno III's wife, Angela, emphasize? a. The speed of the process b. The number of paint cans needed c. Attention to detail d. The size of the paintbrush
4. What is one source of inspiration for color and design ideas mentioned in the guide? a. Watching television b. Reading a novel c. Nature d. Playing video games
5. What is the purpose of a mood board? a. To store leftover paint b. To visualize your color palette and design elements c. To practice painting techniques d. To track your painting progress
6. How does Nicholas Salerno III teach his painting methods? a. Using colored brushes as symbolic awards, similar to martial arts belts b. By focusing solely on speed and efficiency c. By encouraging students to use only one type of paintbrush d. By emphasizing the use of low-quality paint for cost-saving purposes

1. In the mini guide, what is one way to maintain the newly painted exterior of your home? a. Ignore any signs of damage or wear b. Regularly clean and inspect the exterior for signs of wear or damage c. Apply a new coat of paint every month d.

Use water to clean painted surfaces daily

2. What additional topic will be covered in Part 2 of the "Painting Your Beautiful Home" guide? a. Wallpaper and specialty finishes b. Cooking and baking tips c. Gardening and landscaping d. Home improvement projects unrelated to painting

1. Which technique is recommended by Royal Painting for achieving a flawless finish when painting walls and ceilings? a. Cutting in and rolling b. Applying paint with a sponge c. Using a single, thick layer of paint d. Painting without any preparation

2. What should be done with leftover paint after completing a painting project? a. Discard it immediately b. Properly store it for future touch-ups c. Mix it with other paint colors d. Leave it open to dry out

3. When choosing a paint finish for a room with high moisture levels, such as a bathroom, which option is the most appropriate? a. Matte b. Eggshell c. Satin d. Semi-gloss

4. What is the primary purpose of applying primer before painting? a. To increase paint adhesion and durability b. To make the paint color appear darker c. To reduce the number of paint coats required d. To create a textured surface

1. How does the architectural style of your home influence your color and design choices? a. It determines the type of paint you should use b. It affects the harmony and visual appeal of your home c. It has no impact on your color and design choices d. It influences the size of your paintbrush

1. Which of the following is an important step when preparing cabinets for painting? a. Removing doors, drawers, and hardware b. Applying paint directly on top of the old finish c. Avoiding sanding the surfaces d. Skipping the use of primer
2. In the context of interior painting, what is the recommended approach for touching up and fixing imperfections? a. Ignoring imperfections b. Using a different color paint for touch-ups c. Applying an excessive amount of paint to cover imperfections d. Identifying and fixing imperfections with a small brush and matching paint
3. What is a key consideration when selecting the right paint for your home's exterior? a. The paint's ability to resist fading and peeling b. The paint's smell c. The paint's packaging design d. The paint's popularity among neighbors

1. According to Nicholas Salerno III, how does teaching martial arts influence his approach to teaching painting methods? a. It emphasizes the importance of discipline and precision b. It encourages a focus on speed and efficiency c. It highlights the need for constant competition d. It promotes the use of a single paintbrush for all projects
2. What is the primary goal of Royal Painting when it comes to setting industry standards in professional painting? a. To prioritize speed over quality b. To promote the use of low-quality paint and materials c. To consistently achieve beautiful and lasting results d. To focus on the author's personal accomplishments

Answers:

49

1. a
2. d
3. b
4. c
5. c
6. c
7. b
8. c
9. b
10. c
11. c
12. b
13. a
14. b
15. a
16. a
17. b
18. d
19. a
20. b
21. a
22. d
23. a
24. a
25. c

Congratulations for completing this helpful book and test on "Pain*ting Your Beautiful Home: A Comprehensive Mini Guide with Industry Standards by Royal Painting*." By investing your time in this guide and test, you have taken a significant step toward mastering the art of painting and design. Keep practicing and applying the expert advice and techniques shared by **Nicholas Salerno III** and **Royal Painting** to achieve beautiful, professional results in your own home.

"Enjoy the painting process and have fun creating your new space!"

Don't miss out!

Visit the website below and you can sign up to receive emails whenever Nicholas Salerno III publishes a new book. There's no charge and no obligation.

https://books2read.com/r/B-A-KCMK-ILGHC

Connecting independent readers to independent writers.

Did you love *Painting Your Beautiful Home*? Then you should read *The Battle Plan Against Addiction*[1] by Nicholas Salerno III!

[2]

The Battle Plan Against Addiction

Actively help a friend, family member, or loved one fight the battle of addiction. Understanding the addict and addiction. Your role in all this, and reconnecting back to self. Putting together an intervention and getting them the help they need. Coaching, and further assistance. Lots of resources and links to further education on all topics discussed, and much more.

By Nicholas Salerno III

---

1. https://books2read.com/u/31l7Pa

2. https://books2read.com/u/31l7Pa

Also by Nicholas Salerno III

Dude Smith
The Adventures of Dude Smith

PULP Comic
Lady On The Road
The Wanderer (comic/manga)

Robot Girl
Robot Girl "Escape to Paradise"

The fantastic dog adventures of Kudo
The Greatest Dog In The World
Superhero Dog And Friends
The Fantastic dog adventures Of Kudo

The Wanderer
The Wanderer, Saving Paradise

Standalone
Pulp Reader
The Origins of Santa Claus
The Battle Plan Against Addiction
The Scroll Of Elijah
Painting Your Beautiful Home